Original title:
The Search for Meaning… and More Snacks

Copyright © 2025 Creative Arts Management OÜ
All rights reserved.

Author: Lucas Harrington
ISBN HARDBACK: 978-1-80566-126-9
ISBN PAPERBACK: 978-1-80566-421-5

## Treats of Transcendence

In a world of twists and bends,
I ponder life, and where it ends.
But first a crunch, a salty bite,
My quest for truth feels just so right.

Chasing chips through time and space,
I munch and giggle, what a race!
The deep-fried wisdom makes me smile,
With every nibble, I go the extra mile.

Are pretzels fate, or just a snack?
I toss my doubts into a pack.
With each sweet bite I venture near,
To cosmic snacks that bring me cheer.

Popcorn kernels in a bowl,
Crunching answers for my soul.
The munching sounds? They're wise, they say,
Life's just better with snacks on display.

Divine donuts in a heap,
Lost in thought, but still I leap.
As muffins sing their sugary tune,
I find my joy beneath the moon.

## Whims of Wonder

What's the purpose of this quest?
To find the snacks I love the best.
A chip, a dip, a tasty treat,
A journey full of things to eat.

They say that knowledge is the key,
But I prefer a bowl of brie.
With crumbs of wisdom in my hand,
I'll put my thoughts on pizza land.

I'll ponder life while munching fries,
With every bite, a sweet surprise.
Philosophy may be a bore,
But popcorn makes me want to score.

So here I am, with smiles and grins,
In search of fun and cheesy wins.
With snacks galore, I'm feeling fine,
Let wisdom wait, it's snack time shine!

## An Appetite for Understanding

Fill my plate with questions fried,
And toss my doubts aside with pride.
With nachos stacked to reach the sky,
I munch and muse, oh me, oh my!

Why do we crave the hidden truth?
Like chocolate bars, they bring our youth.
But all I want is popcorn's crunch,
As I dive deep in every lunch.

The mysteries of life perplex,
But every cookie here connects.
With each sweet bite, I clear my mind,
And leave my heavy thoughts behind.

So let's indulge, my jurors dear,
In flavors bold, we've nothing to fear.
Understanding will wait its turn,
While tasty bites make my heart yearn!

## Seeking Dishes of Destiny

I wander through this endless hall,
In search of snacks that call my all.
With doughnuts hanging like sweet dreams,
I follow flavor's wild extremes.

What lies ahead, I cannot tell,
But maybe chips with salsa sell.
Life's great purpose in a feast,
As I devour, my joy's released.

I ponder nachos, warm and gooey,
While trying to remain so choosy.
Yet every morsel whispers truth,
In every crunch, I find my youth.

So here I stand, with snacks in hand,
My destiny is crisp and grand.
I'll take a bite, then take a pause,
For every snack's a worthy cause!

## Pondering Over Pretzels

With twists and turns, I navigate,
The salted wonders on my plate.
A pretzel knot, a circle of cheer,
I munch with glee, my thoughts crystal clear.

What does it mean to find the way?
Could it be found in gourmet spray?
Or maybe just in butter's glaze,
As I dip my thoughts in snack-filled haze.

I chew and muse, it all feels right,
For every crunch brings me delight.
With every bite, I laugh and sigh,
What's life without a sweet pie high?

So let's be silly, let's indulge,
In all the flavors that emerge.
While seeking answers, let's make snacks,
For happiness is in the cracks!

## Savoring Silence, One Snack at a Time

In a world of crunch and munch,
I seek the quiet, hear the lunch.
Potato chips whisper, soft and sweet,
While gummy bears dance to a sugary beat.

Almonds meditate, calm and still,
Each taste a treasure, a savory thrill.
Popcorn pops with secrets to share,
In the silence, I find my flair.

## **Palate Pilgrimage**

With every nibble, each thoughtful chew,
I wander through flavors, both old and new.
Chocolate rivers flow, caramel streams,
A snack quest fueled by silly dreams.

From pretzels twisted to nachos supreme,
Every bite bubbles with laughter and cream.
Oh, the joy in each crunchy embrace,
I scout for snacks with a goofy grace.

## **Beyond the Plate: A Quest for Joy**

Adventurous souls in the cupboards roam,
Seeking that popcorn, a forkful of foam.
The quest is silly, the snacks divine,
I chase down cookies, like a red wine.

Pizza rolls pirouette on my dish,
Every crispy bite—my snacktime wish.
In the pantry, I stumble, giggle and trot,
With laughter and crumbs, I've found my pot.

## Munching on Mysteries

What is that flavor hiding in there?
A sprinkle of madness, perhaps a flair?
Chips of unknown origins call my name,
In the munching game, I stake my claim.

Mystery snacks wrapped up tight,
Each one unfolds like sheer delight.
With a crunch and a giggle, I dive right in,
In this snack adventure, I'm sure to win!

## Whispers in the Crumbs

Little crumbs beneath my feet,
Whisper secrets oh so sweet.
What is life without a bite?
Pizza sings in the moonlight.

Fridge of dreams, what do you hold?
Leftover tales, both brave and bold.
Fries of wisdom in a box,
They laugh at me in mismatched socks.

## Ephemeral Feasts

Plates stacked high, but gone so fast,
Moments fleeting, they don't last.
A donut's joke is round and sweet,
As I dance with crumbs beneath my feet.

Chips forgotten, crunches galore,
Salty wisdom I can't ignore.
Burgers chatting over a fry,
Sausage links that wave goodbye.

## Craving Clarity in Chaos

In this chaos, tasty treats,
Find my bliss where sugar beats.
Chocolate bars that softly sing,
Answers hidden in each wing.

Cereal laughs in morning light,
As I ponder the day and night.
Milk spills truths, as frosted flakes,
Conversations with my doughnut makes.

## **Morsels of Existence**

Life is a bag of popcorn puffs,
Full of kernels and tasty stuff.
Bites of joy in silly sips,
Smoothie dreams in fruity trips.

Gummy bears whisper my fate,
With every chomp, they celebrate.
Cake and pie, in playful rows,
Together we embrace our woes.

## Chewing on Life's Questions

In the fridge, a light does glow,
I ponder deep, my snack to know.
Is it chips or a sweet delight?
With each crunch, I feel so right.

What's the meaning of this snack?
Do I share, or keep it back?
With every munch, I contemplate,
What's the answer? It's too late!

## Satiating the Hungry Heart

A heart that yearns for savory cheer,
Found solace in a box of beer.
But wait, what's this? A pizza slice!
I question life; it seems so nice.

With every bite, I feel the bliss,
Should I grab a second? That's the risk!
Finding joy in cheesy layers,
Life's a feast, for hungry players.

## **Bites of Reflection**

Upon my plate, I ponder fate,
A donut's ring—a tasty mate.
Does icing hold the key to joy?
Or is it just a sugary ploy?

I scoop some guac, and I must confess,
Avocado leads to happiness.
With nacho chips and salsa bold,
The meaning's found in guac, I'm told!

## The Quest for Flavorful Truths

In quests for truths, I scour the store,
With snacks galore, who could want more?
A candy bar or maybe fries?
Wisdom wrapped in sweet disguise.

As I munch on these delights,
I ponder all my snack-filled nights.
The flavors dance, oh what a ride,
Life's tastiest secrets, I won't hide.

## Gatherings of Flavor and Thought

At the table of jest and delight,
We ponder our snacks, oh what a sight!
With chips in hand and dip galore,
We muse on life while craving more.

A cookie crumbles, wisdom unfolds,
As we swap stories, the laughter scolds.
'What's the meaning?' we jest in cheer,
'That popcorn's popped and the cake is near!'

Remember the days, all messy and sweet,
When feasts were made from whatever we'd meet?
In boxes and bags, our treasures we'd find,
Fried treasures and laughter, forever entwined.

## Buffet of Beliefs

In the line for wisdom, we pile our plates,
A mix of leafy greens and odd debates.
With dressing drizzled and fries on the side,
What's truth? What's fiction? Let's take a ride!

We serve up confusion with a slice of pie,
With donuts and dreams making spirits fly.
'Is it freedom?' one asks, while munching a roll,
To which we all nod, pretending it's whole.

## **Nibbles of Nostalgia**

In the pantry of time, relics abound,
Were those fries we cherished lost and found?
Old lunch boxes hold secrets untold,
Each nibble a story, a memory bold.

Popcorn tapes and gummy bear cries,
The microwave's hum is our chef's sweet sighs.
As laughter spills over, like soda poured high,
We feast on our past, under nostalgia's sky.

## Relishing Resilience

With chips as our armor and nachos as shields,
We brace for the trials that life often yields.
When the cheese gets messy and we trip on our fate,
We laugh and we crunch, and we just can't wait.

In this banquet of chaos, we find our strength,
With cookies for courage, we go to great lengths.
'When life gives you lemons,' one boldly declared,
'Just make it a party—snacks fully prepared!'

## Snacking on Serendipity

In a world of chips and dips,
I found a quest for bliss,
Between the crunch and munch,
Happiness is hard to miss.

I wandered through the store,
With gummy bears in tow,
In this pursuit of joy,
It's sweet and salty, don't you know?

Each cookie crumb a clue,
To secrets life doth hold,
With every bite a laugh,
And stories yet untold.

So I snack and I giggle,
With ketchup on my fries,
In every little morsel,
Existence meets surprise.

## Flavors That Speak

A pickle and a donut,
What a duo, I must say!
In this dance of flavors,
Who knew they'd want to play?

Cotton candy clouds above,
In a sea of cheese and fun,
Every taste a dialogue,
This feast has just begun.

Chocolate whispers sweetly,
While pretzels laugh along,
In this banquet of delight,
And ketchup sings a song.

So gather 'round the table,
Where snacks make life complete,
In every single flavor,
A friendship we can eat.

## Nutrients for the Mind

With popcorn in my brain,
I ponder life and joy,
Each kernel filled with knowledge,
What a thoughtful ploy!

I munch on granola bars,
As wisdom starts to flow,
These bites of crunchy brilliance,
What more could I bestow?

A nacho filled with insight,
And salsa's spicy flair,
With every tasty morsel,
Intellect fills the air.

So snack, my friends, and ponder,
As you savor every crunch,
In this curious adventure,
Life's questions take the plunge.

## The Palette of Purpose

Like artists with their snacks,
We blend and swirl the tastes,
Each flavor bursts in laughter,
No moment goes to waste.

A scoop of ice cream wisdom,
Sprinkles of delight,
As we create our canvas,
Food art throughout the night.

With caramel drizzled dreams,
And cookies shaped like stars,
The palette of existence,
Is one that truly jars.

So nibble on your passions,
And dip into the fun,
In every tasty moment,
Life's masterpiece is spun.

## A Platter of Possibilities

On the table lies a feast,
Countless snacks from west to east.
With nachos, chips, and dips galore,
What am I searching for?

With every crunch and cheesy bite,
Questions fade with each delight.
Are chips the truth or just a snack?
I munch my way along the track.

Crispy bites and savory pie,
Philosophy or just a fry?
Amidst the crumbs, I ponder deep,
Snack on thoughts while others sleep.

## Sips of Introspection

With each sip of fizzy drink,
I pause to ponder—what do I think?
Is my life a soda pop?
Will I fizz, or will I flop?

Bubbles rise like thoughts in me,
What's my goal? Just let it be!
And when it's flat, do I retreat?
Or grab some snacks and take a seat?

Crisp potato, crunchy joy,
More than just a simple ploy.
Every munch bites into time,
Like nachos dipped in cheesy rhyme.

## Grappling with Grains

A cookie crumbles, thoughts collide,
Oats and flour take a ride.
Do they lead me to the lore?
Or is it just a cookie score?

With gluten swirling in my head,
I snack on wisdom, crumbs instead.
Is bread the path or just a tease?
I chew, I ponder, and then I sneeze!

Granola bars stacked high and tall,
Their destiny, do they hear my call?
Each fiber speaks a hidden truth,
While I rejoice in snack-filled youth.

**The Journey of a Thousand Bites**

A thousand bites to reach the goal,
Do I eat, or does food control?
Each morsel a step on this path,
With snacks to guard against the wrath.

Chocolates whisper, "Take me now!"
Wisdom comes with every chow.
Is that enlightenment I taste?
Or just chips with spicy paste?

The journey's long, the snacks are real,
With every crunch, a little zeal.
This culinary quest, so sweet,
Who knew that munching could be neat?

## Revelations in a Takeout Box

In cardboard confines, wisdom hides,
Fortune cookies, my guide with pride.
I ponder life over sesame seeds,
Chasing answers with fried rice needs.

Noodles twist and turn in fate,
With each slurp, I contemplate.
What is truth, what is real?
Is it hidden in my next meal?

Sweet and sour, tang and zest,
Unwrap my mind, let taste invest.
In every bite, a thought does bloom,
As I devour knowledge with a spoon.

Leftovers whisper late at night,
Telling tales of wrong and right.
In grease-stained wisdom, I unearth,
The funny truths of my own worth.

## Seeking Simplicity in Savory

A crispy chip, a salsa dance,
In every crunch, a second chance.
I dip my thoughts in guac so green,
What does it mean to feast like a queen?

Taste buds sing with happy cheer,
As spicy sauce draws me near.
Life's a taco, messy, but true,
Filling my soul with every chew.

Simplicity wrapped tight in bread,
With saucy whispers softly said.
Perhaps the key's in a slice of pie,
Or a donut's hole as I wonder why.

In buttery layers, I unwind,
Each savory bite, a quest to find.
A laugh, a crunch—a life well-stacked,
In flavors vibrant, my soul intact.

## Flavors of the Soul

With each mustard swirl, my heart expands,
Pickles on the side, life's strange demands.
In every dip, a story flows,
Of laughter, tears, and all that glows.

Pizza slices lead the way,
In cheesy realms where jesters play.
Is happiness a crust or core?
Or nestled deep in the garlic more?

Cotton candy clouds, sweet delight,
Silly dreams in flavors bright.
I wander through a donut hole,
In sugary bliss, I find my role.

Soups simmer secrets in a pot,
In every spoon, the truth I sought.
Life's a buffet—take a chance,
With funny flavors, join the dance!

## **Grains of Understanding**

Oats in a bowl, a humble start,
Mix them right, they warm the heart.
Each grain a question, soft and round,
In breakfast bliss, new thoughts are found.

Rice and beans tell tales of old,
Of cultures rich, and lives bold.
I take a bite, and wisdom flows,
Sprinkled with spice, as laughter grows.

Bread so warm, it breaks the norm,
In crusts of comfort, thoughts transform.
With butter's hug, I contemplate,
Is understanding served on a plate?

In every crumb, a lesson lies,
In simple meals, the truth complies.
So I munch through life, snack in hand,
With grains of wisdom, at my command.

## Craving Kindness Between Bites

In a world of bites both big and small,
I ponder the purpose behind it all.
Chocolate chips wink from a gooey treat,
But a hug from friends is the ultimate feat.

So I munch on chips while seeking delight,
Contemplating life in the dim kitchen light.
Each crumb that falls feels like a wise clue,
Kindness and cookies, my perfect brew.

Is it sugar that drives my endless roam?
Or the laughter that makes my heart feel like home?
With each crunchy morsel, I search for the clue,
That friendship's best served with a cookie too!

## The Longing for Milk and Cookies

In the pantry lurks my heart's true desire,
Cookies and milk—my blissful choir.
As I sip the cream, I ponder this fate,
Is there more to life than snacking on plate?

Dunking away all my existential fears,
With each satisfying crunch, I shed silent tears.
What if the meaning is hidden in cake?
Or perhaps it's fueled by the joy that we make?

Baking and laughing, what sweet little spells,
I'll trade my old worries for chocolate-filled wells.
A sprinkle of joy, a dash of good cheer,
Life's a cookie buffet—let's make that clear!

## **Seekers of Sweetness**

We wander the aisles, our hearts full of dreams,
In search of desserts that taste like sunbeams.
Marshmallows float on clouds made of cream,
A whimsical world that's better than it seems.

In cones and in cakes, we find solace and peace,
Each sugary bite brings a moment's release.
But beyond the fudge is there a greater quest,
For joy and for laughter, that truly feels best?

What's sweeter than frosting, what's richer than pie?
A good belly laugh as the sugar sails by.
With gummy bears' giggles echoing past,
We munch on hope, finding meaning at last!

## Beyond the Crunch: A Culinary Odyssey

In the depths of my kitchen, a quest has begun,
With crumbs on my shirt, I just want some fun.
Beyond the crunch lies the laughter we share,
Each snack has a story—a memory rare.

From popcorn to pretzels, our taste buds align,
As we nibble and ponder what life might define.
Chasing down flavors that tickle the soul,
Together we conquer, as friendship makes us whole.

So grab a potato chip, let's delve into fate,
With snacks in our hands, it's never too late.
In this whimsical journey, we'll wander and taste,
Finding joy in each moment, not one bite to waste!

## Unwrapping Life's Layers

With each peel, a laugh or two,
Hidden bars, dreams come true.
Chocolate nuggets hide from sight,
Joy unwrapped, oh what a bite!

In crumpled bags, the treasures lie,
Crunchy joys that make us sigh.
A sprinkle here, a dash of fun,
Life's a snack, so let's outrun!

We bury doubts in crispy wraps,
While munching loudly, heart enchants.
A nibble soft, a crackle bright,
Snacks ignite our shared delight!

So take a seat, let's peel and chew,
Life's weird layers, nothing new.
Snack on laughter, crisp and bold,
In a world where joy unfolds!

## Finding Comfort in Crunchy Moments

In the midst of a cookie crunch,
We find joy, a perfect lunch.
Chips and giggles piled so high,
Savor them as time flies by!

Crispy quirks and frosty treats,
Silly smiles in savory beats.
Dip your joy in salsa's splash,
Life's a flavor, make it a bash!

Between the bites, we share our tales,
Chirpy laughs, the fun prevails.
Cracker crumbs on our chins we wear,
In every crunch, a moment rare!

With snacks in hand, we raise the cheer,
Finding comfort, holding dear.
In every crunch, a chance to thrive,
Together, we joyously arrive!

## Savoring Subtle Revelations

In every puff, a thought unfolds,
Crispy secrets, stories told.
Popcorn wisdom, kernels bright,
Snack and ponder through the night!

Nibbles lead to giggles shared,
Each dessert bite, the heart prepared.
Sprinkled wishes on cupcakes' cream,
The sweetest layer of a dream!

Chewy bites and frosty swirls,
Unwrap truths that make us twirl.
With cheesy jokes we raise a glee,
Finding fun in mystery!

As we munch through the truth we seek,
Life's soft whispers make us peek.
So grab a snack, it's time to play,
Each flavor finds a goofy way!

## **Dipping into the Deep**

In a bowl of guac, we dive so neat,
Chips and laughter, such a treat!
Salsa swirls, like life's wild dance,
In every dip, we take a chance!

Swirling fables in nacho cheese,
Each crispy bite is sure to please.
We dip our thoughts in creamy fun,
Together, let the good times run!

Smiles are scooped like veggie sticks,
Finding joy in silly tricks.
As we dip our dreams in flair,
Life's a platter, always fair!

So grab a chip, we journey deep,
Through snacks and laughter, secrets keep.
In every bite, the joy we weave,
With friends and snacks, we truly believe!

## Breadcrumbs of Thought

I wandered through my mind, you see,
With crumbs of snacks and laughter, free.
Each thought a chip, a nut, a cheer,
Delightful bites that reappear.

In every corner, flavors blend,
Each munch a choice, no time to spend.
The quest for depth, a silly game,
With breadcrumbs leading back to blame.

My brain a maze of snacky treats,
A savory blend of silly feats.
I ponder deep as I devour,
The meaning lost in pizza power.

Yet as I chew and laugh aloud,
I find my truth within the crowd.
A bag of chips, a burst of fun,
In snacking bliss, I know I've won.

## Enlightened Palate

With every crunch, enlightenment sings,
A chip, a dip, oh what joy it brings!
I muse on life with nachos near,
As flavors dance, I shed a tear.

Each bite a question, crispy and bright,
Salsa spicy, turning wrongs to right.
I dive into cheese, my spirit high,
In pursuit of truth, I dare to try.

The guacamole speaks, so rich and bold,
While pretzels whisper secrets told.
In every packet, wisdom leaps,
As I munch on chips, the laughter keeps.

Some seek the stars, or books on shelves,
But I find answers in crunchy elves.
With hot wings soaring and fries demure,
I taste the meaning, crunchy and pure.

## Divided Heart

In my chest, a pizza pulls,
While salad waves, my will it dulls.
Each slice a passion, fresh and round,
Where is the truth that I have found?

A chocolate bar calls from the shelf,
"Indulge!" it cries, "Just be yourself!"
While veggies fret to take their stand,
A snack attack, the dreams unplanned.

But deep inside, the struggle brews,
As chocolate waits, the lettuce stews.
What snack is right? What snack is wrong?
In munching woes, I sing my song.

Yet laughter rings, the forks are tossed,
In every crumb, no snack is lost.
I'll blend my tastes, my heart's delight,
With chips and sweets, I'll feel alright.

## Finding Joy in Flavored Moments

In the kitchen, joy takes flight,
With every snack, a pure delight.
I sift through bags of wondrous treats,
In crispy layers, life repeats.

Popcorn whispers secrets sweet,
While cookies dance with every beat.
In flavors bold, I find my cheer,
As laughter fills the atmosphere.

I stack the chips, a crunchy tower,
Each bite a joke, a blissful hour.
Sweet and salty, my heart does leap,
In this buffet, I choose to keep.

Moments flavored with fun and glee,
No deeper truths, just snacks with me.
In every bite, a world to roam,
In flavored moments, I feel at home.

## Chips of Contemplation

I ponder life with a bag in hand,
Each chip a question, oh so bland.
I crunch on thoughts, peppered and neat,
With every munch, I find my beat.

The salsa jar nods, wise and thick,
As flavors bloom, their laughter quick.
With guac beside and crunching sounds,
Philosophy within the pounds.

Should I dip here or crunch there first?
In every snack, my mind does burst.
I smile at all the silly takes,
While pondering life's little flakes.

Yet in this feast of joy and cheer,
I find that humor's always near.
Chips and laughter, my truth thus served,\nIn every bite,
my thoughts preserved.

## Beyond the Crunch

In the pantry, treasures hide,
A bag of chips, oh what a find!
Crunchy bites and laughter's cheer,
Snacking's wisdom, crystal clear.

Each chip a tale, a salty jest,
Searching hard, we find the best.
Dip the salsa, spread the guac,
Snack away the ticking clock.

Life's questions fade with nacho cheese,
Chasing answers with crispy ease.
Peanut butter dreams on toast,
In snackland, we can coast!

So raise a snack, let's take a break,
Finding joy in every cake.
Laughing loud, no need to pout,
In munching fun, we hash it out.

## Unearthing Joy in Every Bite

Digging deep for savory treats,
Finding joy in cookie sheets.
Brownies hide with secret flair,
Even veggies can have a pair!

In every crunch, a giggle waits,
Through chocolate rivers, laughter skates.
Each sweet morsel tells a story,
Snack-time shines, we bask in glory.

Gummy bears, the jester's crown,
Tickled tongues won't wear a frown.
Popcorn pops with a cheerful snap,
In the kingdom of kitchy maps.

So grab a plate, let's make a mess,
Happiness is bite-sized bliss.
Snacks unite us, can't you see?
With every munch, we're wild and free!

## A Taste of Purpose

Cereal in the morning light,
Round and crunchy, pure delight.
Spoonfuls swirl, a milky dream,
In every bite, we find our theme.

Cookies crumble with a wink,
Dunking them makes us think.
What's more meaningful than a snack?
Laughing hard and never slack.

Life's a buffet, come take a taste,
No second thoughts, no time to waste.
Finding meaning in each fry,
Chasing joy with every pie.

So let us feast, no need to rush,
Crunching chips, we find our hush.
In silly moments, we ignite,
Purpose served on a plate tonight!

## Nibbles of Insight

A crumbly cookie whispers wise,
With every nibble, the laughter flies.
Chips and salsa, a crunchy cause,
Each bite sparks joy, our brains buzz.

Doritos bring a color blast,
In snacktime's fun, we're unsurpassed.
Scavenger hunts for tasty eats,
In every chip, adventure greets.

Pudding cups with a cherry cheer,
Making meaning, we volunteer.
Grab a spoon, dive into glee,
In the snack quest, we're all free!

So here's to bites that brighten days,
With crispy fun and cheesy ways.
Life's a feast, let's savor more,
In every nibble, wisdom soars.

## Savory Journeys and Sweet Discoveries

In a land where chips do crunch,
And chocolate bars have quite the punch,
I wander wide with munchies near,
In quest of goodies, hold my beer.

From popcorn clouds to candy streams,
I'll savor life in tasty dreams,
With salsa dance on every bite,
My heart, it sings, a pure delight.

Oh, donut holes and cookie dough,
Each snack a tale, a tasty show,
I chart my course on nacho seas,
With pizza sails, I'm hard to please.

So raise your fork and toast the fries,
Each cheesy goodness is a prize,
The journey's wild, the taste is grand,
In snack-filled lands, I take my stand.

## Morsels of Wisdom

In every bite, a lesson lies,
Like how to dodge the veggie fries,
A nugget here, a crouton there,
I munch on truths, without a care.

Chips may crumble but I stand tall,
While cheese dips whisper 'give your all,'
Two scoops of joy, a sprinkle of fun,
Life's surplus flows, like a snack buffet run.

The popcorn pops as laughter grows,
Each kernel teaches things we know,
Like how to dip in guac with flair,
Or spread a cream for anyone to share.

So as I crunch through life's fine meal,
I savor snacks and joy I feel,
With every treat that comes my way,
I find the wisdom in play each day.

## A Tapestry of Taste

In my pantry, colors blend,
A tapestry where flavors send,
Each layer wrapped in foil and dreams,
With zestful dips and zany creams.

Sundaes build with towers proud,
While salty snacks draw quite a crowd,
From burgers stacked to cakes so wide,
A world of joy where taste can glide.

I twirl with pretzels 'round my waist,
Embracing every savory taste,
A sprinkle here, a drizzle there,
Life's great feast is beyond compare.

So plunge into the bowl of fun,
With every bite, let laughter run,
Together, we'll create and share,
This endless plate of love and care.

## Snackable Insights

Crunching thoughts as I retreat,
To find the snack that can't be beat,
Pringles stack like dreams up high,
A salty wave under the sky.

Cookies crumble, wisdom spills,
Between the bites, I pay my bills,
Chocolate leads me down the way,
To find the truth in what I slay.

Each marshmallow a fluffy thought,
In graham crackles, truths are caught,
Pop-tarts guide me through the night,
With icing drizzles, oh what a sight!

So let's indulge, don't hold back now,
For snacking joy deserves a bow,
With every nibble, life is bright,
In every crunch, there's pure delight.

## Seeking the Essence of Every Morsel

In the fridge, the light glows bright,
A snack adventure, pure delight.
Chips and dips, a savory maze,
Searching for joy in crunchy phase.

Midnight cravings call my name,
Popcorn popping, it's no game.
Chocolate bars in secret stash,
Savor each bite, oh what a bash!

In every crunch, a giggle found,
Each little nibble, pure joy abound.
Cheese and crackers, a perfect pair,
Snackin' wisdom, life's little flair.

Embrace the crumbs, don't let them fall,
In each morsel, hear the call.
Life's too short for tasteless fare,
Let's munch and laugh without a care.

## Journey Through Flavor and Thought

In my pantry, treasures hide,
A snack quest, come take a ride.
Tortilla chips and salsa splash,
Brain food found in every stash.

I ponder deep on nacho fate,
With every crunch, I contemplate.
Chocolate cookies, wisdom's friend,
Embrace the crumbs, let the fun extend.

Popcorn kernels, thoughts in flight,
Butter drips, oh what a sight!
As flavors dance in buttery bliss,
Life's big questions wrapped in this.

Each snack savored, laughter shared,
On this journey, well-prepared.
With every bite, I find my muse,
In crinkled bags, I can't refuse.

## Eating Through Illumination.

It starts with chips, then comes the dip,
In snack-time magic, I take a trip.
A bite of cheddar, oh what a thrill,
Each cheesy morsel, a golden spill.

Doughnuts spinning in sugary dreams,
When life is tough, you know what redeems.
Craving cookies, my heart takes flight,
In frosting, I find my true delight.

In gummy bears, wisdom is sweet,
As each one dances, can't be beat.
Snack on, dear friend, the joy you'll find,
In every treat, you'll free your mind.

With laughing bites and silly grins,
Through each delicious moment, the fun begins.
Peanut butter hugs and jelly cheers,
In this banquet of snacks, we taste our years.

## Quest for Crumbs

On a quest beneath the couch,
Hoping for crumbs, like a hungry vouch.
Cereal bits and cookie flakes,
Gems of flavor, oh what it takes!

Through the kitchen, I wander still,
Seeking morsels, a hungry thrill.
Between the cushions, anticipation grows,
Every crumb found is like a rose.

In silent rooms, I munch and crunch,
Sacred snacks devoured for lunch.
A hoard of snacks, my heart's delight,
The mess I make is worth the bite.

So here we are, snackers unite,
In search of joy, not just tonight.
With laughter and crumbs, we'll rule the day,
Snack on, dear friends, we'll find our way.

**Plates of Possibility**

A plate of dreams, piled high,
Tacos and guac, oh my, oh my!
Chasing flavors, bold and bright,
Each bite a giggle, pure delight.

Exploring dips, a treasure hunt,
With every scoop, I boldly stunt.
Nachos whisper, come and play,
Morsels dance, they sway and sway.

Pasta twirls in a saucy whirl,
Meatballs dream of a foodie girl.
Life's a buffet, fill your plate,
In tasty quests, we celebrate.

So grab a fork, and let's embark,
On culinary trails, a flavorful lark.
With humor served and laughter tossed,
In plates of possibility, we are never lost.

## Mourning the Last Chip

Oh, the tragedy, the final bite,
The last chip crumbles, what a sight!
Salsa's left, with ghosts of taste,
A snacktime drama, so misplaced.

Dippers cry, oh chips divine,
Your crunch was music, a perfect line.
We gather round, a somber crew,
Memories linger, each chip we chew.

So raise a toast, a crispy cheer,
To flavors past, we hold so dear.
In the kingdom of snacks, we shed no tears,
For chips will come again, my dears.

Let's savor all, while we're still here,
With nacho tales, we'll share our cheer.
In every crunch, we find our way,
To laughter and joy, come what may.

## Finding Light Among the Appetizers

In the dim light, a tray appears,
Brimming with bites, we toast our cheers.
Spring rolls giggle, while olives wink,
Magic lies in each savory link.

Bruschetta sings of tomatoes bright,
A chorus of flavors, pure delight.
Finding friendship in hummus dips,
We share our stories, and playful quips.

With skewers dancing, here's the game,
"Who eats the most?" we stake our claim.
In this banquet of joy, we unite,
Amidst laughter and snacks, all feels right.

From cheese cubes to mini quiches,
A feast of fun, fulfilling wishes.
In every bite, a story's spun,
Finding joy in each snack, we've won!

## Slices of Solitude

In quiet corners, pizzas call,
A slice for me, a feast, not small.
Cheesy whispers, crusts that cheer,
In solitude, I find my beer.

With every pepperoni laid,
Thoughts of loneliness start to fade.
In marinara, dreams do float,
On this tasty, savory boat.

Craving snacks, my heart's delight,
On pizza's crust, I take my flight.
In each bite, solace I find,
A joyful heart, a playful mind.

So let the world outside pass by,
With every crust, I touch the sky.
In solitude, I snack and dream,
In every slice, I find my theme.

## Unwrapping Layers of Existence

Beneath the foil, secrets hide,
Chocolate dreams, my trusty guide.
While pondering life's great quest,
I nibble snacks, my heart at rest.

With each bite, I find my way,
Crunching truths in a fun array.
Potato chips or cookies sweet,
In every morsel, life's a treat.

So unwrap layers, snack away,
Laugh at thoughts that try to stay.
Existence may be quite absurd,
But chocolate-covered joy's the word.

In every crinkle, in every crunch,
Philosophy reveals its hunch.
As I munch on cheesy puffs,
I rethink life—who needs the fluff?

**Flavors of Reflection**

Popcorn kernels flying high,
Thoughts like butter rush and sigh.
Savory shades of salty grace,
Still, I can't find my true place.

Between the bites of nacho chips,
Philosophy ties my thoughts in grips.
Do I dip? Or just partake?
In every flavor, I'm awake.

The salsa sizzles on my tongue,
Contemplations getting young.
As spicy thoughts ignite my mind,
I search for snacks of every kind.

Munching kale or fruity snack,
Life's a journey, never lack.
With each flavor, I find delight,
Reflecting on the cosmic bite.

## **Enlightenment in Every Bite**

In every crunch, wisdom might hide,
Potato skins, my trusty guide.
As I dive deep in snack-filled sights,
I ponder truths amidst the bites.

Grains of popcorn, kernels of thought,
Salty snacks that life forgot.
Between the crunch and gooey cheese,
I find my answers with such ease.

The wisdom flows like melted goo,
In every cheesy, crunching stew.
I chew on life, both sweet and wild,
In crispy joys, I'm like a child.

A donut hole, a waffle vague,
Enlightenment in every plague.
For each snack reveals what's true,
Maximize flavor, let joy ensue!

## The Road to Raspberry Jam

A spoonful of joy, a smear of bliss,
On toast of life, there's much to miss.
I navigate this tasty road,
With raspberry dreams, I'll lighten my load.

Beneath the jars, old truths await,
We spread our hopes; we contemplate.
Is it the bread or the jam divine?
In every bite, a twist in time.

Chewy gummies, or maybe spread,
Life's a buffet, never dread.
Every layer, a thought to jam,
The meaning of life in every slam.

So as I sit with spoons aligned,
I laugh alone—what truth I find!
With jam and bread, I claim my day,
For joy is here, so let's not stray.

# The Last Cookie's Meaning

In the jar, it stands alone,
A cookie shrouded in sweet tones.
What secrets does it hide inside?
A crunch of tales, a sugary ride.

Should I savor it in slow bites?
Or devour it, in wild delights?
A last crumb dance on the floor,
Will it share its tales of yore?

It's baked with joy, it seems, this treat,
But can it make my life complete?
As I ponder, the clock does tick,
Should I wait or go for the quick?

Breaking it apart with haste,
I find it whispers, "Life's a taste."
So with a smile, I take that leap,
And laugh as I indulge and keep.

## Savory Questions in a Sweet World

Why is broccoli dressed in cheese?
Does it think it's here to please?
Carrots wearing coats of dip,
Are they on a flavor trip?

Chips and dips have tales to tell,
In this crunchy, munchy shell.
Do they ponder too, at night?
In the pantry devoid of light?

Popcorn pops with questions galore,
"Why do people love me more?"
As I munch, I smile and nod,
These snacks are wise; I can't applaud!

In a sugar coat, the world seems fine,
But salt has layers too, divine.
So I snack and laugh away the doubts,
In this savory maze, let's twist about!

## Analyzing the Appetizer

Tiny bites that steal the show,
What mysteries do they bestow?
A brisket bite with hints of spice,
Is it deep or just a slice?

Velvet dips, oh creamy dreams,
Navigating through cheesy themes.
Can an olive hold the key,
To finding joy in savory glee?

A bruschetta topped with flair,
Asks if life can be laid bare.
Do they ponder with each bite,
"Are we more than mere delight?"

So as I munch and slice away,
The appetizers seem to say,
Life's a platter, round and wide,
Taste it fully, let's not hide!

# Munching on Memories

Chips and salsa, a past packed tight,
Recall my youth in every bite.
Nachos stacked, so tall they sway,
Is nostalgia the cheese today?

A pizza slice brings back our dreams,
Of late-night talks and silly schemes.
Garlic knots whisper tales of old,
In buttery warmth, our laughs unfold.

Popcorn crunch in dim-lit rooms,
As we share our favorite tunes.
Each kernel a gem of laughter shared,
In a bowl of memories, we dared.

With every crunch, a story's spun,
In snacks of life, we find the fun.
So as I savor every bite,
I munch on memories, pure delight!

## **Hungry for Wholeness**

With an empty plate, I roam,
I munch on dreams, far from home.
Seeking answers in each bite,
Crunchy wisdom, day and night.

A buffet of thoughts piled high,
Joking with fries, oh me, oh my!
Life's a feast, or so they say,
But where's that vegan cake today?

## **Digesting New Ideas**

Chewing on thoughts, I take a chance,
Mixed flavors in an awkward dance.
Spicy truth, a hint of mint,
Laughter bubbles, won't give a hint.

Cereal philosophies, oh so bright,
Puffed up insights, such a delight.
Pouring milk on musings galore,
Keep 'em crunchy, never a bore!

## Banquet of Beliefs

At the table of thoughts, I sit,
Hopes sprinkled like sweet chocolate wit.
A stew of wishes, odd and neat,
Sipping soup while tapping my feet.

Gather round, everyone, let's feast,
On laughter, joy—a never-ending beast!
Salad of dreams, tossed with care,
With croutons of love, shared everywhere.

## Stacking the Snacks of Solitude

In the corner, I stack my chips,
With nacho wisdom, 'til the dip slips.
Piled high with solitude's embrace,
Crispy crumbles fill the space.

Popcorn thoughts burst with a bang,
Sipping soda as silence sang.
Alone but happy, in my snack zone,
Each crunch a laugh, I'm never alone.

## Quest for the Perfect Bite

In gardens of flavors, I roam and I seek,
A chip with a crunch that will make my heart squeak.
With salsa, or guac, or just plain cheese dust,
I dive into snacks, with fervor and trust.

A donut-filled dream, a brownie to chase,
I nibble my way through this curious space.
Yet life feels so bland without savory crunch,
I'm lost in this quest for the perfect lunch.

Each morsel a laugh, each flavor a song,
In puddles of cheese, where I truly belong.
With pickles and snacks, my dilemmas are few,
Just one more potato chip—oh, make that two!

As I munch through the mess, I ponder and sigh,
Is it love that I taste or just ranch on the side?
In laughter and crumbs, my spirit takes flight,
Forever I'll quest for that heavenly bite!

## The Snack of Existence

Sitting alone with my bowl of warm peas,
I ponder the mysteries—oh, where is the cheese?
A sandwich, a taco, or pasta delight,
Existence is tasty, but where's the good night?

The universe stretches like a gummy bear's form,
With nachos and pudding, how can I stay warm?
As I sip on my soda, bubbles like dreams,
It's snacks that give meaning to life, or so it seems.

Yet whispers of veggies creep into my mind,
Though salad might help, what joy can I find?
With croutons like treasure and ranch on the side,
Do they hold all the answers? I'm filled with such pride!

So pull up a chair and join in my feast,
Let's crack open chips, for the joy it released.
In laughter and munching, let worries depart,
For snacks are the true way to nourish the heart!

## A Spice of Discovery

In cupboards I rummage, exploring the shelf,
Seasoning my musings with a dash of self.
Oregano whispers, cinnamon calls,
As I sprinkle my thoughts on coconut balls.

Each crunch of the cracker, a trail I will blaze,
With sprinkles of chaos and savory haze.
An apple, a cookie, or some peanut delight,
What hidden wisdom lies just out of sight?

I fry up my hopes with a side of despair,
Zucchini and fries scatter, friends in the air.
The flavor of joy, or is that just salt?
In buttery bliss, I loosen that vault.

So dance with the spices, let laughter unfold,
In cheesy confessions, bright stories retold.
For the zest of our journey mixes sweet with the tough,
And snacks make it clear: we're simply enough!

## Chewing Over Contemplation

In the depths of my ponder, I gnaw on some gum,
Thinking of life's question, how'd snacks come from?
With popcorn as solace and jellybeans sweet,
I'm caught in a spiral of chew, crunch, repeat.

Each crunch makes me wonder, each dip brings a smile,
Is it chips that are wise, or just me for a while?
A cupcake of wisdom, a pie full of grace,
In this banquet of snacks, I've found my true place.

The chocolate is melting, the cookie is crunched,
As I ponder the cosmos, my thoughts feel quite hunched.
Yet, cookies remind me, life's tasty and round,
For when I am munching, true joy can be found.

So grab a snack buddy, let's dive into fate,
Together we'll savor, let's celebrate late.
In the crunch of our banter, a slice of delight,
The meaning is clear: let's munch through the night!

## Feasting on Forgotten Dreams

In the pantry, visions stew,
A banquet of hopes all askew.
Chips in hand, I take a bite,
Chasing shadows, what a sight!

Each cookie crumbles like my plans,
A dance of crumbs, my sweet demands.
Still I munch, though dreams may fade,
With every crunch, my fears evade.

Like pizza slices lost in time,
I savor each cheesy rhyme.
Nibbles on the edge of fate,
Snack attack, oh how it's great!

From doughnuts to forlorn desire,
Each sprinkle's a taste of the fire.
Life's buffet with treats galore,
I'll feast forever, craving more!

## Taste Buds and Truths

My tongue's a compass, drifting wide,
In flavors deep, I take my ride.
A jalapeño bursts with glee,
Revealing secrets, spicy spree!

Gummy bears hold wisdom strange,
In every chew, they rearrange.
Salty nuts share mysteries,
As laughter echoes with the breeze.

In the candy aisle, wisdom's flair,
A chocolate bar, do I dare?
Crunchy bites unveil life's jest,
With every snack, I feel so blessed.

So grab a plate, let's all unwind,
With pastries sweet and cheeses kind.
Life's absurd, like caramel's pull,
With every taste, my heart is full!

## Gathering Around the Snack Table

In the glow of the snack-lit night,
Friends all gather, what a sight!
Popcorn rivers, cheese galore,
Who needs a menu? We want more!

Chips are crunched, like laughter flies,
In every bite, a small surprise.
Jokes are tossed like peanut balls,
Snack brigade, no room for stalls!

Pretzels twist with wisdom great,
Crackers carry tales of fate.
Together munching, hearts ignite,
Sharing snacks feels so just right.

As the clock ticks, we raise a toast,
To joys found in the tiniest most.
Here's to friendship and the feast,
In every crunch, life's joys increased!

## Crumbs of Connection

In every flake, our stories blend,
Tiny crumbs of time we send.
Pizza remnants, laughter loud,
In this feast, we're all so proud.

Sipping soda from the can,
Secrets shared with every plan.
A cupcake holds a dream or two,
In frosting swirls, our lives anew.

Sudden spills bring giggles near,
Melting marshmallows chase the fear.
In messy bites, our soul's unveiled,
Through sticky fingers, we've prevailed.

So let us feast, let troubles slide,
With snacks as our trusty guide.
In every crunch, we bond and cheer,
Life's best moments always near!

## The Hidden Depths of Dough

In a world of yeast and rolls,
We ponder life while munching bowls.
Soft pretzels twist, like fate's own hand,
Thus, comfort food makes us feel so grand.

Pizza slices, wide and bright,
Topping dreams on every bite.
Each crust a journey, warm and gold,
Within each bite, a story told.

Bagels circle without an end,
With every schmear, we can pretend.
A quest for truth in every spread,
But maybe it's just cheese instead!

So let's explore each flaky treat,
With laughter as our favorite beat.
In each bite a giggle waits,
Snack on, my friends, before it's late!

## In Pursuit of Flavorful Truths

Chasing flavors, a tasty chase,
Lost in crumbs, I find my place.
Chips and guac, a savory lie,
With every crunch, my spirits fly.

Salsa dances, fresh and bright,
While nachos gleam under the light.
Questions swirl like spicy zest,
In this feast, I feel the best.

Dips and bites, a merry crew,
Each morsel whispers: here's to you!
With every snack, I find my muse,
Tastes of life I cannot refuse.

On this platter, wisdom awaits,
Witty banter fills the plates.
In savory seekings, joy's found,
With every nibble, truth unbound!

## Revelations with Every Nibble

Each nibble brings a giggle near,
As chocolate drips and thoughts are clear.
A cookie's crunch, sweet life's delight,
In round bites of joy, all feels right.

Marshmallows fluff like dreams do soar,
Roasting over flames, we crave for more.
With each s'more, lessons unfold,
In gooey layers, wisdom's gold.

Fritters fry in bubbling cheer,
A taste of life, and oh so dear!
French fries whisper salty quests,
In every crunch, delicious tests.

So gather round this tasty scheme,
Snacking on the edge of a dream.
In every morsel's joyous sass,
Find laughter, love, and snacks en masse!

## Crumbs on the Path to Enlightenment

On a path strewn with crumbly bits,
Snack attacks make the mind do flips.
With popcorn popping, birds take flight,
In buttery dreams, all feels right.

Donuts glazed like life's sweet spree,
Each bite a loop, a mystery.
With sprinkles bright, wisdom's fate,
Savoring moments, don't hesitate.

Tiny cakes of every hue,
Muffins bursting with thoughts brand new.
With frosting swirls, I chase the sun,
In frosting fights, we all have fun.

So stroll this path of frosted treats,
Sharing laughter and lovely eats.
Enlightenment in every spoon,
Snack your way beneath the moon!

## Whispers in the Cracker Box

In a cupboard high, they scheme and plot,
A chorus of crackers, their flavor gang caught.
'Cheddar or sour? Which one do we bake?'
An existential crisis, oh what a mistake!

A peanut butter jar jumps in the fray,
'I'm versatile, try me in a new way!'
And out of the shadows a fig jam appears,
To spread out the doubts and calm all the fears.

## Appetites of the Soul

With a chips and salsa kinda vibe,
Life's flavors serve as our tribe.
Nacho cheese dreams in a guacamole haze,
Craving connection through toasted maze!

Calories counting, what's the cost?
In piles of popcorn, we've never lost.
Pretzels twist thoughts, bring laughter and light,
Snack with purpose, our futures are bright!

## Digging for Purpose in Potato Chips

With each crunch we seek, what lies beneath?
Barbecue or plain? Whisper the wreath.
The answer lies hidden in salty delight,
Among the crumbs and joy, we find our bite.

Flavors collide, like fate in a bowl,
Every nibble uncovers a piece of the soul.
Ketchup or mustard, it's quite the affair,
In this crunchy quest, nothing can compare!

## A Journey in Every Flavor

Exploring life through tortilla twists,
Searching for meaning in zesty risks.
Salsa spills secrets, brings friends together,
Life's a feast, let's snack, whatever the weather!

Ice cream dreams swirl, a sweet serenade,
Dancing with joy in a crinkle cascade.
Each flavor a story, each bite a new tale,
Through snacks and laughter, we shall prevail!

## **Feast of Epiphanies**

In the pantry, I dive deep,
With chips and thoughts, no time for sleep.
Each crunch a clue, a tasty sign,
Are snacks the answer? Divine design!

Carrots whisper, 'We're good for you!'
But potato chips have a stronger woo.
Salads mock with leafy grace,
But nachos dance, a spicy embrace!

Morsels of wisdom, sprinkled and fried,
Unwrap the joy, let's take a ride.
Laughter erupts with every bite,
Who knew enlightenment could taste so right?

Join this feast for souls and snacks,
With pudding cups and cheeky pacts.
A banquet of thoughts, frivolous and grand,
In this tasty wonderland, we make our stand!

**Seeking Snacks and Wisdom**

With a rumble in my tummy, I'm off,
Searching for snacks with a playful scoff.
When wisdom eludes, and hunger's near,
Perhaps a donut could lend an ear?

Chips of knowledge, oh so crisp,
Dip them in laughs, let's take a risk.
Pretzels twist with stories to share,
While gummy bears float in a sugary air.

In the cereal box, lies the truth,
Frosted flakes hold the key to youth.
With every bite, I ponder and chew,
Can munching be the path to anew?

So as I snack and ponder the fate,
I find life's joy on my dinner plate.
For in each morsel, a lesson shines,
Between bites of laughter, wisdom entwines.

## Fables with a Side of Chips

Once upon a crunch, tales unfold,
Where chips share secrets and truths bold.
A salsa saga of flavor and zest,
Each dip a story, each bite a jest.

In the land of sweets, the cookies chatter,
With icing on top, it's all a matter.
But gummy worms want to steal the show,
As epic tales of salty flows.

The popcorn pops, wisdom takes flight,
Telling tales of brilliant insight.
With a pat on the back, a toast to the fun,
Stories are best when snacks are begun!

So gather 'round for a feast of delight,
Unwrap your fables, enjoy the bite.
For in every crunch lies a magic spun,
Life's lessons served, under a setting sun.

## Gathering Crumbs of Knowledge

In the corner lies wisdom, crumbs of delight,
Scattered with laughter, a curious sight.
From chocolate bars to cookies so sweet,
Each bite of knowledge is hard to beat.

I nibble on thoughts 'neath the fridge's hum,
With every snack, I become less glum.
Where chips declare wisdom loud and clear,
And caramel drizzles away all fear.

As gummy bears sing their sugary songs,
I jot down notes, the night feels long.
With cupcakes nearby, I savor the quest,
For snacks and knowledge—oh, what a fest!

So here's to the crumbs that lead us to fate,
In chocolate sprinkles we celebrate.
With every munch, let wisdom grow,
In this quirky journey, let happiness flow!

## Salty Questions

In the pantry, I stand and stare,
Wondering what's lurking everywhere.
Chips and crackers ask the deep,
Where's the wisdom, or should I eat?

Pretzels twist with a knowing grin,
Do they hold secrets, or just salt within?
I ponder life over popcorn fluff,
Are snacks my guide, or just plain stuff?

Beneath the crunch, thoughts dive and dive,
Do munchies inspire, or just keep us alive?
Candy wrappers whisper, 'Take a chance,'
As I battle hunger in a tasty dance.

So many treats in this cosmic grab,
Do they hint at purpose or just make me drab?
As I chomp on chips, I think and chew,
Is my mind deeper than a bowl of goo?

## **Sweet Answers**

Marshmallows float in the land of delight,
Chasing giggles and dreams every night.
Chocolate's promise wraps me in warmth,
But is wisdom in bites, or a candy storm?

Cookies crumble with a crunch so fine,
Do they share secrets or just taste divine?
Frosting swirls hold mysteries bold,
Is the truth layered thick or just painted gold?

Lollipops spin in a colorful whirl,
Do they have answers or just make me twirl?
Every sugary bite, a puzzle to solve,
As I ponder if cravings help me evolve.

So I munch on my treats with playful cheer,
Finding sweet solace, the meaning's near.
With every bite, laughter and love,
Perhaps the truth fits just like a glove.

## Craving Context

Fridge full of wonders, I gaze in awe,
Searching for purpose in food's every flaw.
Leftover pizza sighs with a plea,
Do you hide answers, or just calories?

Granola bars crunch with wisdom untold,
Are they the mysteries that life has sold?
Nut butter whispers, 'Spread me around,'
But do I find secrets in what's being browned?

The sandwich waits, a tale to unfold,
Does it speak truths or just lettuce cold?
Tacos stacked high, a flavorful mess,
In each bite, do I feel more or less?

With every tasty morsel that passes my lips,
I question the thoughts as the crunchy trip slips.
Finding context in crumbs, laughter, and bliss,
In every snack moment, I find my own twist.

## Unpacking Life's Delicacies

The picnic spread is a sight to behold,
As I unwrap layers of stories untold.
Syrupy drizzles dance in the sun,
Is this how life's meaning is packaged and spun?

Cheese boards offer flavors, both sharp and sweet,
Do they map out journeys I'm yet to meet?
With crackers as guides, I nibble and muse,
Is enlightenment served with a side of blues?

Fruit medleys burst, a colorful crew,
Each bite a lesson, each flavor so true.
Do grapes' laughter hint at tomorrow's quest,
As I load up my plate, I search for the zest?

So I feast with my friends on this platter of fate,
In every slice shared, we contemplate.
Are conversations richer than the food on our hands?
With each cheesy bite, together we stand.

## Crusts of Contentment

Warm bread rests, a loaf of delight,
Comforting crusts hug me snug and tight.
As I chew on the edge, questions arise,
Is joy found in bites or in friendly ties?

Croissants whisper secrets in flaky lines,
The butter's soft touch, a friendship that shines.
With each gentle munch, I wonder aloud,
Is happiness baked in, or lost in the crowd?

Bagels provide purpose, a circle of care,
I ponder the meaning while toasting to share.
With toppings galore, each one a delight,
Can we spread truths with a savory bite?

As I savor the crusts, warmth fills my soul,
These baked-up moments make anyone whole.
Perhaps life's best answers lie under the crust,
In sharing our snacks, in laughter we trust.